DOUG TIMES

DOUG TIMES

ELEVEN MEMORABLE DAYS
THAT POSITIVELY IMPACTED MY LIFE

JOHN SNELL

WINDY CITY

PUBLISHERS

DOUG TIMES
ELEVEN MEMORABLE DAYS THAT POSITIVELY IMPACTED MY LIFE

Windy City Publishers
2118 Plum Grove Road, #349
Rolling Meadows, IL 60008

www.windycitypublishers.com

Published in the United States of America

ISBN#:
978-1-941478-84-4

Library of Congress Control Number:
2019912336

WINDY CITY PUBLISHERS
CHICAGO

PREFACE

In the 1950s and '60s, when life was innocent in Harwood Heights near Chicago, Illinois, the thoughts and actions of my neighborhood friends were typically youthful, yet respectful. My friends and I were all about the same age except for our friend, Douglas "Doug" S. Lind. Doug was several years older and we looked up to him. He was a servant leader if there ever was one, before "servant leader" was a common reference. We did not know what it was that made him so creative and likable, but in retrospect, Doug's single most noticeable characteristic was his noble character. He had concern for others, both adults and us younger kids. We followed him through his life's adventures. His life became our lives.

We grew up on his block on Oconto Avenue. Foster Avenue was the western boundary and Carmen Avenue was the eastern. The houses in our neighborhood were small and recently built. Our gang of kids was Doug, George, Skipper, and me, John. Sometimes George's sister Lanie, my sister Juil, or Skip's sister Donna would tag along on our adventures.

We were from poor families, although we did not realize this until we were much older. The adventures and memorable experiences of our lives on the block were directed, like a master conductor, by Doug. Some of the most notable and fun adventures of my youth are recounted in this book.

Doug was about four years older than the rest of us, except Lanie who was one year older than George. Doug was a gangly fellow who had bony hands and feet, wore glasses, had black hair and green eyes, and was noticeably taller than all of us and many kids his age. George was small, chubby, and cute. Lanie was attractive and looked like her mother, with long light brown hair and brown eyes. Skipper was the handsome one; tall with dark hair and brown eyes. I was the skinny one, with light brown hair and brown eyes. My sister Juil had light brown hair and blue eyes, and was beautiful. I used to tease her a lot. Donna was the gorgeous blond, with a good personality.

We all worshiped Doug.

I want to thank Pennoyer School, the Burlington Historical Society, NAS Glenview Museum, and Cox Company. Thanks to my sister Juil, and others who helped steer the time machine; Carol Lind King, who gave her expert advice to keep Doug alive and provided proof-reading, my son Johnny with his keen sense of the present, and my wife Mary, my soul mate and cheerleader. Thanks to the good folks at Windy City Publishers, especially Lise, Dawn, and Ruth.

These were Doug Times. Enjoy as I did.

CHAPTER ONE

NEW SHOES

There are days when I do not want to be outside playing, or be outside at all. Most of the time I would rather be inside my house reading comic books, or maybe even doing homework. In the 1950s, we do not have much homework. Time at school is more about learning about life, recess twice a day, and modeling yourself after a teacher you admire, one of the cowboys on TV, or another boy in the neighborhood than it is about learning reading, writing, and arithmetic. But the risk of being inside is that I am available to be assigned to run errands, to do chores or other menial labor, and to help my mother. On one particular Saturday, early in the morning, Mother asks me to run an errand.

"Johnny, are you there?" she says.

I know I am being considered for some errand by the tone of her voice.

It used to be that when we needed milk it would be delivered right to our house. I would look out the living room window when the milkman pulled up on Oconto Avenue. He drove a small white truck which he parked along the curb in the street, near the driveway. This gained him direct access to our property without walking on the grass while he carried glass milk bottles to our back porch. He dressed in a white outfit and hat and went about his business very quietly. Mom would anticipate his schedule because the milk did not stand on the porch very long. But milk delivery days were over.

The new National Tea store has recently opened at Foster and Harlem, about a block away from our house. Being so close to the house, it is now easy to send your son over to get milk or groceries. Mom wants me to get two gallons of milk. She must have plans to bake something good. I lament, "Goodbye, Mr. Milkman."

While Mom is looking for some cash in the drawer next to the silverware drawer, I spot Doug, George, Skipper, and Lanie through the open blinds on the dining room window. They are slowly walking on the sidewalk in front of my house, headed for our front door. I hear, "Yo, Johnny," followed by some shouting and laughing. They can see me inside through the living room window. I take the cash from my mom, roll it up tight in a wad, and put it into the front pocket of my jeans. I open the front door and hop down the front stairs into the front yard to join them.

My mom says, "If your friends want to go with you, that's fine."

Doug says, "Where are you headed JT?" I love it when he calls me JT.

"Gotta go to buy some milk," I say quietly.

I sense they would rather be doing something other than going to the food store with me. I am wrong. Doug has an ulterior motive. He has a plan. I think I know what he is up to, and I think the others do too. Doug, as usual, takes the lead with a grin. We all walk together to the National Tea store on the concrete sidewalk on the south side of Foster Avenue. George gripes a little because it is early in the morning.

"George, you baby," Lanie says. George is not a morning person. His sister teases him for it. Most importantly, we are all happy to be together.

We head east toward Harlem Avenue. We cut through the empty lot behind the National Tea store on a well-worn trail. The parking lot, with its surface of dirty brown gravel, is about a hundred feet long and equally wide. It makes a great playground. There's a small sign posted at each of the two driveway entrance points stating that the lot is for National Tea customers only. I never noticed the signs before. I figure we can play in the parking lot because I am going to buy some milk, and that, by definition, makes me a customer of National Tea.

Once we enter the parking lot we are running around between parking lanes and jumping on and off parking bumpers like we usually do. I am with George, jumping from bumper to bumper in the parking spaces near the front of the lot along Harlem Avenue. The bumpers are wood timbers about twelve inches by twelve inches and maybe about eight feet long, located at the front of each parking space. They are all painted yellow to enhance their visibility. It is pretty easy even for eight-year-olds to jump from the end of one timber to the end of the other, then run down the timber bumper and keep on jumping. Naturally, we stay away from parked cars that prevent us from our jumping activities. At this time there are only four cars parked in the lot, and they are parked at the corner, near the entrance to the store, away from where we are playing. While George and I think we are making some good time, we look up to see Doug, Skipper, and Lanie, almost to the end of the parking lot towards the back of the store.

"Let's go, George. We're getting behind," I say.

Then it happens.

The sound of passing traffic now and then and the sound of a lonely car pulling into the gravel parking lot are interrupted by a shout from our hero, Doug. It is a cry of pain. We freeze to see where he is and what is going on. It does not look pretty from my vantage point, even half a parking lot away. We all run to Doug, who is standing near the end of a yellow timber bumper. He looks around at us running toward him. He looks at his foot. He does not move.

In the few seconds it takes for us to reach him, we see him looking at his foot and then to us and then back at his foot. As I get close I notice a large rusty nail coming out of the top of his right shoe about where the ball of his foot should be. It does not look good. Also, they are new shoes; dark brown boat shoes with white soles sprouting real leather ties on top. They are slip ons. The closer I get the more it looks like we are going to be headed to the hospital. It does look like Doug is injured, the way he his holding his ankle, but there is no blood. None.

Then, Doug realizes he cannot play act any longer. As he grins and looks at me, with a twinkle in his eye, he slowly slips his bare foot out of his damaged right shoe. The shoe stays firmly attached to the yellow bumper, but his foot is fine. He explains that he had jumped onto the end of the timber and accidentally landed on the nail with his right foot. Being the blessed guy he is, the nail went through the sole of his right shoe, between his big toe and second toe, and popped out about an inch or so from the top of his shoe. After some detailed inspection, we see that the big ugly rusted nail is sticking upright out of that yellow timber. Doug pulls the shoe off the nail and puts it on his foot. We find out later, the next time we see him, that he got in big trouble from his dad and mom for ruining his brand-new shoes.

After all of the excitement, we all go into the store to pick out the two newest-looking milk bottles. They look like the ones the milkman used to deliver. We patiently, but with giggles, stand in line to pay for them and leave the store and the parking lot behind. We also leave the rusty nail behind. Doug proudly carries both bottles of milk home to my house and presents them to my mom.

Later that same day, Doug takes his dad's sledge hammer on the sly and pounds the big rusty nail sideways into the timber bumper. Doug is protecting us so our jumping fun will be safe for the next time.

Doug, his Mom, his Dad, and Whiskers the cat.

CHAPTER TWO

ROCKET

It is late on a Friday afternoon. I am sitting on my front porch, which is an unusual event for me, since I like to be inside my house. Doug is walking by on the way to his house, five lots down Oconto, with two bags of groceries, closely following behind his mom. While he is walking by he looks at me and says quietly, "Hey, JT, come over tomorrow morning." I give a feeble but understanding wave of my right hand.

Then his mother says, "Hello there Johnny. Say hi to your mom and dad," to which I reply, "Hi Mrs. Lind. I will."

You see, there are some Saturdays that Mrs. Lind makes it all the way from the National Tea to the sidewalk in front of our house carrying two bulky paper bags of groceries herself, without Doug. She appears around nine in the morning, before the heat of the summer cooks the concrete sidewalks and makes even walking a sweaty workout. In these cases, I usually see her, or worse, my mom sees her first and volunteers my services. Either way I would ask her if I could carry the two bags, never more than two, that she was carrying. She would always gladly accept my offer. When I got to her house and dropped the bags on her kitchen counter, she'd give me a cookie (homemade, of course), but the real satisfaction was that I got to do my Boy Scout good turn for the day.

Doug's parents and my parents did not hang out together and rarely saw each other, but were good neighbors. In our neighborhood it seemed that every parent or adult who lived on our block contributed to my and the other Oconto Gang kids' upbringing, particularly those adults who were parents.

I learned much later from my mother, when Doug was serving in the Air Force, that Mrs. Lind had had diabetes most of her adult life. I felt good knowing that way back when I helped her carry her bags of groceries, I got to do an especially good deed.

After watching Doug and his mom walk down Oconto and turn up their driveway, I then sit down on the top step of the front porch to dream about what Doug has in store for tomorrow. Before going to bed this night, I open the window at the head of my bed maybe two to three inches, as I usually do in the summer to listen to traffic on Foster before I fall asleep. It is therapeutic to hear gears shifting and engines revving, even at nine years old.

I wake up face down with my left arm over the edge of the bed, partly uncovered, with the north wind moaning through the screen of the bedroom window. My hand hits my nightstand, a small wooden barrel I use for holding my Boy Scout stuff, on its way up to scratch my nose. I yawn deeply. Putting on a T-shirt, underwear, jeans, and sneakers is automatic, keeping the other side of my brain available to be excited about what Doug has in store for today.

"Mom, I am going to Doug's," I shout as I leap down the front stairs and run down the sidewalk to Doug's house. Today would be a no-bikes day, a walking-only day. As I approach his house, he is on his front porch waiting for me. He grins and waves. It perks me up. As I step up the one step from the sidewalk to his house he asks if I've had breakfast and I admit I haven't. "See you in the back yard," he shouts, and goes into his house through the front door. I round the corner of his house, where his brother keeps his partially completed home-made sailboat in the gravel driveway just outside the garage. The garage door is open. Doug must want to build something. I am now waiting in the back-yard. It is getting to be a long time. I am discouraged. Then he jumps over the railing from the porch that is the exit from the kitchen, holding two folded paper towels.

"Breakfast," he says.

Inside my paper towel are two slices of seeded rye toast painted thickly between with crunchy peanut butter: a toasted peanut butter sandwich. Doug made the same for himself. I never have had this kind of breakfast before. He knows I like crunchy peanut butter. I start to eat right away. Both of our tasty treats are gone in about twenty seconds. The peanut butter completely sticks to the roof of my mouth.

It would not be the only surprise for me today.

We look at each other, well satisfied.

Doug asks, "You like it?"

"Yup," I replied nervously.

"OK," Doug says.

On the work bench in the garage, next to his father's tools, are a piece of one-inch by four-inch wood, about a foot long, and a half-built plastic model kit of a dragster.

"Hey, JT, help me attach these wheels." Then he pauses and says, "No, not now. I've got a better idea." Looking away, he focuses on a small metal object on the bench amongst a myriad of old tools. He picks it up. It is a spent cartridge from an air gun. He calls it a CO_2 cartridge. The magical tubular piece is about three inches long, has a restricted opening on one end, and is closed on the other. Doug shouts, "Yo, George," from his yard and in a couple of seconds, George comes flying out of his house next door, over his concrete sidewalk, asphalt driveway, and low hedge (or what is left of it), between their properties. He must have been watching us. I feel good because I got the peanut butter on rye toast and George didn't.

Doug then asks both of us to go home and bring him a book of paper matches. That is an easy one for me since my dad smokes. I run home. I know my dad has matches in the drawer next to the sink in the kitchen and also in the basement, on his workbench. When I arrive back at Doug's garage, he and George are not there. They are sitting on George's front porch, tearing the heads off each paper match from several books and dropping them into the cartridge.

"Hey. I got a book," I say, approaching the porch.

Lanie, George's big sister, is there too, ripping off match heads. I start too, with the cartridge about half full. We are running out of matches. Doug gets another book from his house. Now we are carefully placing the last match heads in the cartridge, with Doug placing a cotton ball in the orifice to hold the matches in. None of us except Doug knows what is going on.

Then he shouts, "You guys stay here, and if anybody asks you what you are doing, say nothing." We are team brothers at this point and we want to complete the top-secret mission. He gives me the cartridge. Then he heads for his garage. It is a long time before he reappears, maybe ten minutes. He is holding a long aluminum tube. We can tell Doug has something intense planned for today. It will be something we have never done before, and we are excited. The day is energizing to us kids.

Doug has drilled a small hole in the tube about one half inch from the bottom, all of the way through. The dull gray tube is slightly larger in diameter than the cartridge, so that the cartridge slides easily down the tube, with room to spare, but is prevented from falling out of the tube by a small nail inserted through the tube in the two holes.

We are all feeling giddy because we have made this thing, but Doug is the only one who knows what it can do. The constricted end of the cartridge pro-trudes neatly out of the bottom of the tube, which is about four feet long. Next, Doug looks for a proper ground zero launch site. The prairie across the street from my house is safe, with no adults around, so Doug heads that way, and of course we follow, not knowing what a thrilling event is about to occur. The prairie becomes our perfect launch site. It is a flat piece of prime real estate which will soon become a shopping center, but for now it is our big and undeveloped prairie. We talk about other good times playing in the prairie. Everything looks normal to any observer, since all that can be seen are a short metal pipe and four good-looking kids crossing Foster into the prairie.

We are doing what has to be done, since it is getting near lunch time. We must complete the mission before one of us is called home. That would prob-ably be me, since my house is across Foster from the prairie.

Doug is organizing the launch as best he can. Doug chooses George to hold the tube, with two hands, in vertical orientation. The cartridge is supported on the nail at the bottom of the tube. The cotton extends out of the bottom of the cartridge, about one inch or so below the bottom end of the tube. Doug chooses me to light the cotton. As I strike the match, a long wooden one from the box Doug brought for this occasion, I wait.

Doug says, "Well go ahead, what are you are waiting for?" Really, I did not know, but a little fear of the unknown creeps into my thoughts. I do not respond. The match goes out. After the previous hesitation, this time to appear gung-ho, I strike another match and quickly light the cotton. The rest of the story is seared into all of our brains.

A loud explosion, red fire exiting out the bottom of the aluminum tube, hot white smoke, the rattling of the cartridge going up the tube at many feet per second, and George holding on for dear life, yelling out something, and the rest of us shaking in fear—all of this was not caught on film but should have been. We created something that only Doug knew would be as exciting as it was. Doug made this happen hoping to impress us kids. He sure did. When the rocket left the tube, because of its size, natural gray color, and high velocity, the cartridge could not be seen in flight. Had we planned to be able to see it in flight maybe we would have painted it red or yellow, or yellow with red stripes, but even that would not have helped. In our anticipation of what would occur and the excitement during the launch we did not see the cartridge in flight. We never found it.

To us little kids, the experience of launching a rocket was terrifying. We never talked about the rocket again.

CHAPTER THREE

LYE

In Chicago the summers can be very hot. In the evening the night air cools down some, so I open the window at the head of my bed before I hit the sack. This week it seems that each day is as hot as the next. My dad says there is no rain in the weather forecast for the next week. He is a little on edge because of the extended dry spell.

It is early Saturday morning, and my dad has his routine. He is making pancakes, from scratch, for my sister Juil and me. Then mom can sleep in on Saturdays. However, without a doubt, when she wakes up she gets pancakes too. We have thick, dark corn syrup with the blue label and a fresh stick of butter to give the meal real style. We always have butter. No oleo. Our family, as well as all of our relatives, uses only butter. To this day I do not know why. This day I hear my mom say that Uncle Bill, her younger and only brother, and his wife Pauline, are using oleo. I think my mother is going to cry, but she doesn't.

This morning the pancakes are as good as it gets. No wonder: my dad, when he cooks his pancakes, always uses bacon grease. I am going on my third one when I hear Doug, George, and Skipper in the back yard. No trouble, just Doug probably with some plan for the day. I can't make out what he is saying. The last pancake disappears when my sister takes it off the platter and puts it on her plate. She loads it with syrup and begins to eat. The commotion of my friends in the back yard has my concentration, not Juil taking the last pancake. Although it does bother me, as her big brother.

"Dad, I am out of here with Doug, George, and Skipper. Thanks for the great pancakes," I say.

Dad says, "OK, JT. Back at lunch time."

Juil just waves her fork at me, and I am out the back door, down the back porch steps, past the garbage can and into our back yard. I brush against the small hedge on the south property line separating our property from the Flynns'. I run over the little concrete and stone patio, pass the garage on the east, and go around the small garden behind the garage on our southern property line.

When I round the corner of the garage, I see them there, Doug holding George's head under his arm, George faking being choked: always kidding around.

Doug says, "Let's go into the prairie." Yes, the same prairie that was ground zero for our rocket launch. He must be feeling adventurous today, since the prairie is shared by our gang, the Oconto Gang, and the North Side Gang from the housing project north of the prairie. We never really fight each other except maybe a punch here and there, but nothing serious.

Today will be different.

We four boys walk across Foster Avenue towards the prairie. There is little traffic so we do not need to look both ways. We are the Oconto Gang. My front porch watches us disappear into the high grass and into a grove of small trees. I am starting to feel the heat. It is getting hot. It is mid-morning. So far, no sign of the North Side Gang. This is good. We press on through the tall grass to the east side of the pond, which is our turf.

Things look different from the last time we were here. A large area is now cleared, with evidence of some construction going on. There are piles of construction materials such as concrete blocks, bags of concrete, bricks, and a few shovels. Our playing in the prairie will soon be coming to an end, but we do not care. Playing around the construction materials is fun too. We look to see if anybody is around. Nobody is there. We are alone. It is getting hotter.

Then, we hear the sound of boys, which may be the North Side Gang tramping through the prairie. It is. The North Side Gang comes into sight. They do not see us yet. Doug looks around at the construction material, which can provide some cover for us. The other gang is coming closer. He tells us to quietly and quickly get out of sight behind a large pile of concrete blocks. From the sound of their talking to each other they still do not know we are there. Doug's plan is to surprise them. He tells us to get ready. He does not tell us what he has planned, but we find out when he jumps up, stands on another small pile of concrete blocks and shouts, "Hey, get out of our prairie!"

"No. You're in our prairie," Will, their so-called leader—a short, heavyset blond boy—shouts back.

Doug says, "Just you and me, Will. Leave the others out of it." George, Skip, and I look at each other with disbelief. It looks like Doug wants a fight. He must have got up on the wrong side of the bed today.

Will looks bewildered, but manages to shout back, "OK, big shot." The "big shot" remark makes Doug angry. Now he is ready for a fight. He quickly jumps down from his perch on the concrete block pile and lands in a puddle of soupy mortar mix. That makes him even madder. Will thinks this is funny. Doug's new shoes, the pair that replaced the shoe damaged by the nail, are covered in yucky white mortar. That was that.

Doug shouts, "Will, you stay where you are and I will stay where I am. You and I are in a war. Both feet on the ground and nobody moves." The three of us kids start to move out from behind the pile of concrete block to get a better view of the upcoming war. We are trying to get a good view but also try to stay out of the way of flying mortar.

Will, being close to a large mass of mortar, unexpectedly picks up a handful and heaves it toward Doug. Doug dances out of the way but keeps both feet on the soft gooey ground. Now it's Doug's turn. He bends down, grabs a handful of mortar, oozing between his fingers, as we watch at a safe distance. Doug is tall, and older than Will. He can really throw a football and baseball well. He gets into passing configuration and lets his handful fly. It hits Will on the shoulder, with most of the white mixture running down his chest. That's one. Now it's Will's turn. He hits Doug on his jeans just above the ankle.

It's late morning with no shade. It is really hot. We are all sweating. They keep throwing handfuls of mortar at each other, every minute or so. There is mortar all over the ground around and between them. The throwing lasts a long time, maybe thirty minutes or so. Will is mostly covered in mortar. Doug has mortar on his jeans and his shoes. Doug is a good shot. Will is not. Will decides it is over—does not announce it, but just leaves. He shouts at his gang members who have been watching and heads through the prairie, out of sight, towards the red brick houses to the north. It is a long walk after his defeat.

Two weeks later, our band of kids, the Oconto Gang—this time with Lanie, George's older sister and Donna, Skipper's younger sister—is playing in the west end of the prairie, down near a new and very large foundation. It is the beginning of the construction of a new Jewel supermarket. In addition to the Jewel, there will soon be construction of an immense shopping mall.

Doug challenges us to walk on top of the one-foot-wide hard concrete foundation walls that are in place. The height of the wall on average is ten feet above the adjacent excavated ground. The planks used by the concrete workers to gain access to the inside of the foundation are leaning at a steep angle on the top of the foundation wall and extend to the ground outside the foundation wall. They make excellent ramps for access to the top of the foundation wall: great fun for kids. Of course, Doug leads the way.

We slowly make progress around the top of the foundation wall. On the west side of the foundation we see the church my family attends, St. James Lutheran Church, now that the woods on the west side of the prairie have been cut down. Pastor Johnson is outside the fellowship hall doing some weeding. He gets up to shout at us to get down off the wall. I hope he is far enough away that he does not recognize me. Following Doug, we carefully avoid stepping on the bent-over rebar on the top of the one-foot-wide wall. Accidentally nudging one of those rebars with your foot means down in the hole you go, or at least a cut on the ankle. Fortunately, we are careful and nobody falls into the gaping foundation hole, or gets a cut ankle. We finish our walk around the top of the wall, on the east side, at the slanted wood plank where we started. I am glad to walk down the plank from the high wall onto solid ground.

Then we look to the east to see someone coming toward us.

Because most of the vegetation, except for a few very large trees on the large piece of property that had been our prairie, is now cleared, it is easy to see from where we are, at the new foundation for the Jewel supermarket, all the way to Harlem Avenue on the east end. We see a small boy at the far end walking towards us. It's Will, or Lye, as Doug has nicknamed him after the mortar war because of the lime in the mortar.

Doug pulls up the leg of his jeans and shows us his ankle. We see a brown patch, where the mortar burned his skin before he could get home and scrub it. He tells us his skin was burned by the chemical makeup of lime, or lye, in the mortar.

Lye is getting closer. He is headed right at us kids. After Doug's little lesson on the effects of the lime in mortar we notice Lye's discolored, angry face. Also, his legs show brown spots below his shorts and his neck reveals the same discoloration above his T-shirt. It is unusual to see him alone, without his gang, but here he comes. He slows his pace as he gets closer. He is now about ten feet away from us. We are all a little sick from his appearance.

He says to Doug, "You did this."

Doug says, "It was a fair fight. Don't blame me. You had the same chance of hitting me. Go home. Leave us alone."

Then Lye says, "I got in a lot of trouble and ruined my clothes too."

Doug responds, "Yeah, I really got into trouble too. I ruined another pair of my new shoes, you dummy."

There is no other conversation. They both stare at each other for a second or two. Then Lye retreats toward the red brick houses to the north. We are all, including Doug, ready to call it quits and go home, so we do. We cross Foster at Osceola and each of us heads directly home to report in to our parents. Another exciting adventure with Doug comes to a close.

But there is more to come.

I do not see Lye, or any of his gang, for a long time. Until one day, after school on a Friday. I am parking my new, three-speed, red Schwinn bicycle with chrome fenders and red and white saddle bags—a fine bicycle, which my parents bought me for my birthday—in front of the fabric store in the new shopping center, now built and occupied with tenants. No more prairie. Mom had asked me to go to the store to buy some thread for her. As I put down my kickstand I notice, in my side view mirror, Lye and several members of his gang walking down the shopping center sidewalk, perhaps fifty feet away. They do not know I can see them. Lye still bears a few of the same scars on his face, neck, and legs from the mortar fight with Doug.

After parking my bike on the sidewalk I enter the store to make my purchase. I come out of the store with a small brown paper bag in which there are three spools of thread. Before I get on my bike, I notice a large wad of spit on the beautiful two-tone red-and-white seat of my new bike. I am sure the spit is from Lye and his awful gang. I look around but do not see anyone. Also, I am sure they are watching to see what I will do. I question in my mind what

I should do. Then it hits me: Do what Doug would do. The spools of thread are in a paper bag. I remove the spools of thread from the bag and put them in my left saddle bag. I use the paper bag to wipe the gob of spit off my seat. Because the bag is made of paper, it works pretty well. I dispose of the wet paper bag in a trash receptacle nearby, get on my bike, ride off, and leave this disgusting experience behind me. Fortunately, I never see Lye or any of his gang again.

CHAPTER FOUR

FLYING RACE CAR

Another beautiful fall Saturday arrives on the block. I wake to hear the wind rustling the leaves in the large elm tree outside my bedroom window. My bedroom is on the north side of my house on the second floor, overlooking Foster Avenue. The air smells fresh. It is early and there is little traffic on Foster Avenue. After getting dressed I join my sister Juil, who woke up earlier and arrived in the kitchen before me.

"Hey, Juil," I tease as I reach down to pet Calico, our cat.

Juil grins. Calico meows. Dad is making pancakes. My sister and I enjoy sitting down to yet another pancake breakfast compliments of our Dad. After my fill of my Dad's pancakes I am ready for another day of playing with my friends. But nobody comes over. Nobody shouts, "Yo, Johnny."

Without telling my dad or mom, Juil and I leave the house, which puts us both in hot water. We go through the front door, hop down the front porch stairs, and run down the sidewalk on Oconto to Doug's house. His house is about halfway down the block, next to and just before we get to George's house. Even though it is not a race I get to Doug's house first. We stop at the end of his driveway at the sidewalk. I look down the driveway past Doug's older brother's almost-finished and built-from-scratch sailboat to see Doug in the garage behind his house, working on some project very early in the morning. It seems that he usually has some project either on the drawing board or under construction.

As Juil and I approach he has a scowl on his face like we are interrupting him and his work. He pushes his glasses up on his nose and looks at us. Juil is particularly upset. I tell her to stay here, even though she wants to leave. We are both watching Doug trying to install a new wood propeller on a Cox 049 Babe Bee model airplane engine. He tells us the wood propeller will not work.

He says he will have to make a special propeller. We do not know what he is talking about.

He then motions to his father's work bench. Lying on the bench is a wooden, model car about twelve inches long, painted red, custom designed by Doug. A thing of beauty. It has large rubber tires on shiny plastic wheels from a model kit and a streamlined body Doug made from a solid block of wood. Both Juil and I respect Doug's expertise in building models. I have learned a lot about building models from Doug.

The problem is that the standard wood propeller is too big when it's mounted on the platform on the wood body. He looks at us and we see that scowl again. He is acting oddly intense and Juil does not like it. His mind is working overtime to come up with a design for a smaller yet powerful propeller that he can make himself to provide the necessary thrust. He is now heading to the scrap pile behind his garage, a rather large collection of various sizes of wood, steel parts, and scrap metal, which is partially overgrown by weeds and uncut grass. Juil and I follow him. He finds a small strip of aluminum sheet, probably from some old flashing.

"Help me pull this one out," Doug says. The three of us pull hard on the corner of a piece of aluminum at the bottom of the pile. After we pull it completely out Doug says, "This should do it," as we follow him back into the friendly confines of the garage.

Mrs. Lind, who knows when it is time for a break, calls out to Juil and me from the back porch, which is no more than ten feet from the garage, to come in for cookies. Doug, still intent on his work, motions for us to go into the house. We do not hesitate. We know her cookies are terrific.

After thanking Mrs. Lind for the cookies, we leave the house and return to the garage, bringing a cookie out for Doug. The cookie removes the scowl from his face. He starts to carefully cut the aluminum sheet into a square about 4 inches by 4 inches. This will be the template for his handmade propeller. After some drilling, cutting, and bending, he attaches the four-blade aluminum creation to the 049, which is now mounted to the work bench. To test the motor and blade assembly he adds gas to the engine and gives the aluminum propeller a flick of his wrist. It starts right away. Doug tells us it is a new engine his older brother bought for him. The sound of the Babe Bee is quite loud. Juil holds her ears. I am tingling all over. He checks the thrust with the back of his hand, nods his head up and down, finally pinches the fuel line, and in short order the motor stops. He smiles and becomes the Doug we are used to having around us.

"Well done, JT!" he shouts. "Let's put this flying race car together."

Quickly, Doug unfastens the mounting screws, detaches the motor with its aluminum handmade propeller from the work bench, and hands it to me for safe keeping. He scrambles for tools and a couple of wood screws he'd previously set aside for the purpose of mounting the engine to the body of the flying race car. In less than a minute the 049, fully work-bench tested by Douglas Lind, is fastened to the race car body. Really, this flying race car is a race car wood platform powered by a model airplane engine. Pretty cool. However, the design phase is not over until the completed project undergoes a field test. A test run down the driveway awaits us.

First, Mrs. Lind invites us with Doug to have a ham sandwich and a cold drink for a quick lunch. It is a ham sandwich piled high with cheese and mustard, like one would find in a classy delicatessen. It is a good break that we share under the shade of the elm tree in Doug's back yard near the garage. We all thank Mrs. Lind for her kindness to us.

Doug's father is home and the family car, a 1954 Dodge Coronet, is sitting in the driveway. Doug's dad is asleep, having worked the previous evening. He is a bus driver for the Chicago Transit Authority. There goes the test run. It will be impossible with the car in Doug's driveway, but there is no car in George's driveway and George's driveway is asphalt, not gravel. Without hesitation, Doug says, "Let's get George involved."

Since George lives right next door to Doug, we all walk on the well worn path through the small hedge which is planted along the joint property line between the adjacent properties. When we get to George's back porch we all yell in unison, "Yo, George," as loud as we can. George's mother appears at the back door.

"George, it's Doug, John and Juil." I imagine George jumping up and quickly getting his shoes on. He flies out the back door.

Doug says, "We need your driveway."

"Huh, what for?" says George.

"You'll see," Doug responds, and motions for all of us to see the flying race car in his garage. "We need to test it and my driveway is full," says Doug.

"Ok," says George. "Let's do it."

We all laugh as Doug carries the beauty to George's driveway for a test run. Having added a little gas to the motor Doug is sure it will make it down the entire length of drive, about 50 feet or so. We are crouched near George's back porch with the flying race car pointed down the asphalt driveway, which is slightly sloped toward the street. Doug asks me to hold the front of the car while he starts the 049.

"Three, two, one," he counts, and with a flick of his finger the motor starts and the propeller whines. I let go. It starts slowly at first, but accelerates quickly. Another problem: Without any control on board the car runs a curved course, turning to the right, slamming up against the exposed foundation of George's house. Doug runs to shut off the motor, which is still running since the car is still upright and pinned against the hard-concrete foundation wall. No damage, but more design issues.

Doug comments that the torque from the spinning propeller is causing the car to lean and veer to the side. It is not understood by us kids.

He says, "We need a string line to control the direction of this thing. Who has string?" We all look at each other.

"I do," we all respond. Then we all set off running as fast as we can to our houses. I go to my kite-string drawer in my room to find an unopened spool of kite string. What a find. *The flying race car project will not fail*, I say to myself. I never ran faster than on my way back to Doug's garage.

When I get back George already has provided his string and he and Doug are setting up the control string in George's driveway. My house is the farthest away. Doug provides an automobile wheel at one end near George's back porch and another near the front sidewalk to hold the ends of the string. Since everything is set up I look at Juil and put my string ball in my pocket. Boy, did I miss out on things.

Doug stretches the string to make sure it is tight. While I was gone getting string, Doug had attached shiny steel eyelets to the bottom of the wood body of the flying race car. These eyelets will be attached to the tight string and will be the guides to keep the flying race car on course. They are open eyelets, so Doug slips them over the string and places the flying race car on the ground at the porch end of the string facing down George's driveway.

It seems that word has gotten around somehow that this flying race car project is about to be launched. Doug's mom is there. Doug's dad, having been awakened by all the noise, is looking out the second-floor window overlooking George's driveway. My dad is there. He reminds me that both Juil and I are in trouble for leaving the house that morning without telling him where we were going. Skipper and his sister Donna, Jerry Indra from across the street, and George's mom and dad, along with his sister Lanie, are standing in the shade near the end of the string line by the street. Doug really hopes this project is a success. So does everyone.

Doug asks me to hold the front of the flying race car as he again flicks the propeller to start the 049. "Three, two, one," he says. He flicks his finger on the crazy-looking aluminum propeller and the mighty little engine responds. The aluminum propeller comes to life as the car wants to move. I let go. I get my hand out of the way of the propeller. The flying race car accelerates down the driveway in about five seconds. It stays on course following the kite string being pulled through the eyelets on the bottom of the frame. What a show.

It then stops abruptly when it hits the steel wheel which stops the car but not the engine. The car is now sitting near the front sidewalk of George's house. Everybody cheers. Doug, Juil, and I run down the driveway and jump up and down. Doug crimps the fuel line and the engine stops. What a day this has been. After the initial run, Doug refills the engine with fuel and proceeds to make several other runs. We all watch each run with amazement and appreciation for the things our hero Doug has created. What we all notice is how Doug involves the kids around him in his success.

As the sun is setting we all say good bye to each other and go home feeling good about our day. Doug takes the flying race car to his room and puts it on the shelf above his bed, along with the many other models he has built. I imagine Doug will sleep well tonight.

CHAPTER FIVE

BALL HAWK

Doug lives in a little blue and white house close to the middle of the block on Oconto. Not surprisingly, all the houses on Oconto are small. They were built after the Second World War to be affordable for returning veterans. However, all of the houses on Oconto and their yards of grass, shrubs, and trees are very well-kept. Of all the houses on Oconto, his house is one of the only ones with a street light on a pole out front, compliments of Commonwealth Edison. The street light gives us kids a location and good reason to stay out after dark even though staying out after dark is a rare occurrence. When we are playing late in the day, our parents are keen to call out to us just before dark to come home. Somehow staying out after dark is a problem for our parents. However, there are evenings when we are allowed to play games like hide and seek in the dark when there is no school the next day, but only around the light pole near Doug's house.

It is another nice spring day. Both George and Skipper are in Catholic Elementary School. Doug is in high school at Maine East. I am in a public elementary school, Pennoyer School. This is the first year in the new building on Cumberland Avenue. The new building is about two miles from my house. I ride the school bus, which stops right in front of my house, to and from school every day. Pennoyer School used to be in the old red brick VFW building on Canfield Avenue, which was a couple of blocks away. I liked the VFW building better.

It is Friday afternoon and I am in school.

I am in English class. Today, instead of our usual English subjects—reading, writing, grammar and other stuff—we are having a spelling bee. I'm not much for spelling bees. This time a prize is being offered. I am sure I will not win. I never do. The boy winner and the girl winner will each receive a gold, spiral-bound notebook and a new pen to go with it.

As usual, because my last name starts with the letter "S," I am near the end of any group activity that depends on alphabetical order. Today, because Wendy Wendt is absent, I am the last participant in the spelling bee. Also, as usual, Steven, the boy genius in our fifth-grade class, has defeated all the other boys before I even get my chance, and as usual Cristina, the girl genius, is leading the girls.

It is now about three o'clock, since the spelling bee is running late. Class is supposed to be over at three o'clock. Mrs. Gardner, the school principal, is looking through the window in the door from the hallway as I am finally called to stand and join the spelling bee. I am looking at Steven and he looks smug as usual, but more so since I am the last hope for the boys. I am not one of the good students. As I said before, I am sure I will not win. I get out of my desk and walk to the front of the class. As I stand there looking at my classmates, Mrs. Slatto, our teacher, says, "The word is doughnut." Great. I know the doughnut shop on Harlem and its large roof-top mounted sign "Donuts" by heart. This will be a breeze. My dejection turns to euphoria. Georgiana, the girl I like in my class, who sits in front of me, will be impressed.

So of course I say, "Doughnut, D O N U T," out loud with determination, in a voice designed to beat Steven. Then I stand there to hear Mrs. Slatto's response.

"That is wrong, John. The word is spelled D O U G H N U T." I am the only one surprised in the room, I think. All I can do is shake my head, feel dejected and return to my seat. Mrs. Gardner, the school principal and a friend of my mom's, witnesses the third-rate performance. Steven gets the new gold notebook and pen. He deserves it.

I am very quiet on the bus ride home. When the bus stops to let me off, I am sad, and I sigh out loud. I walk slowly to my front door, enter my house, and climb even more slowly up the stairs to my room. As I drop my books on my desk I drop onto my bed. I stare out the window at the head of my bed. The wind is blowing through the very large elm tree outside my bedroom window. As I watch the leaves shake and hear the sound of the wind, I imagine pitching for the Cubs tomorrow in their game against the Cardinals. My dream is interrupted. I hear "Yo Johnny" at the back door. It is Skipper. What does he want? Then I think that it is better to get up, stop lying in bed, stop looking out the window and stop dreaming about pitching for the Cubs. That will never happen.

I shout out as I am jumping down the stairs, "I'm coming. Wait Skip wait!" As I open the back door I see him walking down Oconto toward Doug's house. He has his mitt and softball under his arm. My mood is kind of changing, so I pull back into my house to go down the stairs to the basement to get my mitt. It is not a new or good mitt, but it does the job. Skip goes to Catholic school so he was not in my class to witness my spelling fiasco. This afternoon may turn out to be good after all.

As I catch up to Skipper he smiles and says, "Let's catch fly balls. Let's get Doug."

As we get to Doug's house we hear Doug talking with his older brother Harold. We cannot make out what they are saying but the conversation is punctuated with laughter. We hardly ever see Harold, since he does not live at Doug's house any more. He is going to college somewhere.

Skip and I both shout, "Yo, Doug!"

We hear Doug say, "Skip and Johnny, wait for us." So we wait. He must have seen our mitts because when he and his brother come through their front door they have Doug's bat and four softballs. Yes! I almost forget about the spelling bee. We are playing fly ball this afternoon.

When we play fly ball Doug stands in front of the Stocking's house and we kids stand in front of Doug's house near the light pole. This layout works well when it starts to get dark. We can usually see pretty well under the light pole. Little do we know this will be a night to remember.

Harold hits the first fly ball as high as I have ever seen a fly ball hit. Doug catches it. Doug throws the ball back to his brother with his typical throwing form. He throws like a professional ball player. Harold catches the ball on two bounces in one hand while holding the bat in the other. Things are looking good right now. Then, with all of the activity in the street, George comes out of his house with his mitt, ready to go. Things are getting better. So here we are: Doug, Skipper, George, and me in the street waiting to catch fly balls, really high flying fly balls, from Doug's brother. It does not get any better than this. Harold keeps hitting monstrous fly balls. We catch them with ease as long as they do not fly into the trees that line Oconto on both sides of the street.

The day is coming to an end. It is getting cooler. It is slowly getting darker. Then the street light goes on. We all look at each other and expect the worst. We are waiting for calls from our parents to come in for the night. However, the calls do not come, the fly balls keep coming, and so we play on into the darkness.

Then the night falls. The sun has set behind the trees on Oconto. The only light to be seen is from the street light in front of Doug's house.

Doug says, "Harold, this next one will be the last fly ball."

Harold nods, "OK, brother."

The last fly ball indeed. We can barely see Harold standing in the middle of Oconto, even with the orange sky still glowing behind him, through the black shadows of the trees. The air feels cool. In the coolness I wait with everyone else for the last fly ball. I pound my mitt. Harold swings and hits the softball. The ball is a monster high ball, headed for the trees in front of Doug's house right near the light pole. The ball hits one branch at the top of a large maple tree, then another branch, and takes what seems like minutes to respond to gravity. I see George standing by himself near the base of the light pole with one foot in the concrete gutter and the other on the asphalt pavement. We all wait with our mitts ready to catch the ball as it works its way through the maple tree. George has his mitt in the air with this arm outstretched as high as possible. Of all of us kids George is the shortest and youngest. He is wearing a white tee shirt, which sets off his black hair, and dirty blue jeans. There he stands not knowing that the ball ricocheting down the tree limbs is headed like an incoming guided missile, directly at him.

Then the ball makes a last diversion at a sturdy low branch and drops hard on the top of George's head. As the ball makes a thud sound it bounces in the air off the top of George's hairy head and lands in his mitt. At the same time George passes out cold. He falls limply to the asphalt. When he hits the hard asphalt surface, his mitt and the ball go flying into Doug's front yard. Doug and I, who are the closest to him in the darkened street lit only by the pole-mounted light fixture, run over to see about George's condition after his fall and the knock on the head. When we get over to him Doug gently touches him on the cheek. That was enough to wake him up.

George says, "What happened?" Doug looks at me and stares for a second, trying to think of what to say.

Then he carefully responds, "You are the ball hawk. You made a once-in-a-lifetime catch. Nice going ball hawk." George is very groggy when he says to Doug, "I'm the ball hawk?" Doug and I both nod, *yes*.

CHAPTER SIX

LONGEST KITE STRING IN THE WORLD

The Chicago area is well known for its very windy weather conditions. It is even referred to as the "Windy City." Today, a gusty spring day without a cloud in the sky, is no exception. Another Saturday with nothing to do; homework is not a problem. In fact, the generation—my generation—that put a man on the moon, had in general very little homework to do. How about that?

This glorious Saturday, my Aunt Florence is taking me in her new 1956 Cadillac to the mall called Old Orchard. She wants to buy me two pairs of shoes for school, since she, like me, abhors the shoes my mother bought for me. She is technically my mother's aunt, so she can call the shots. My mother never argues with Aunt Florence about anything. It is unusual to me that my mother, strong willed as she is, buckles in any confrontation with Aunt Florence. And, so she will with the two new pair of shoes.

I cannot imagine my mother as a child. I have been told that during the Depression her father and mother lost their house. Their children, including my mother, were sent to live with relatives. My mom as a child lived with Aunt Florence for many years. But that is another story.

At Old Orchard Mall, which offers high quality shopping and is a beautiful place, we stop at the Marshall Fields and Company store. It is a really nice store. She has taken me to the Marshall Fields in downtown Chicago on many occasions. It is also very nice. Going at Christmas time to the downtown store, shopping for toys and eating at the restaurant in the store is a real treat for me.

At Marshall Fields, I notice a section amongst the toys that has kites. The newest ones are not paper, but are plastic with wood supports. They are expensive, though. There is a yellow one that I like a lot, on display. It is made by Hi-Flier. It has distinctive black lettering and a big black airplane printed on the front. I think this one is cool, and besides, Hi-Flier makes the best kites. I stare at the floor for awhile to compose myself, to not appear anxious.

Then I ask, "Aunt Florence, can I have a new kite? My old one got tore up." Aunt Florence and her husband Jack are wealthy and usually buy expensive things for Juil and me. You see, they do not have any children. Both Juil and I try not to take advantage of this situation.

In response she says, "That would be fine Johnny. Which color do you want?"

"Yellow," I say.

"Then pick one out, young man." Without hesitation and with my heart rapidly beating I pick out the yellow plastic Hi-Flier kite carefully wrapped and packaged for sale. She walks up to the counter and pays for the kite. The lady at the counter is very pleasant and smiles at me. I cannot wait to get home.

Several hours later we arrive at my house. I am particularly proud of my new kite, and also my new shoes. Both pairs are slip-on boots. Very cool for young men. I know my mother is not pleased with them so I let Aunt Florence handle that matter with my mom. Aunt Florence wins the battle, as I expected.

Then, my mom says, "You know Johnny, Doug and Skipper were over here this morning. You may want to hook up with them."

"OK," I say, making my way out the front door with my kite. I leave Mom and her aunt to talk. The last thing I hear is my aunt calling my mother by her name, June, so I know she is pulling rank on her. Now I am running down Oconto to Doug's house, holding my new kite for dear life.

When I arrive at Doug's house, Doug, George, and Skipper are sitting together on Doug's front porch.

Doug smiles and says, "What you got there, Johnny?" He asks even though he knows what it is. Ever the creative one, he is already thinking of how and where we are going to launch the kite. Everybody is impressed that I have a plastic kite and not a run-of-the-mill paper one. I silently thank Aunt Florence. Then Doug says, "We can get this baby way up there, without it breaking. It's one of those new plastic kites." So now we know the plan.

"Everybody go home and get as much string as you can, and meet me at Johnny's house," Doug says.

We split up on a run back to our respective houses. This time I have an advantage in that the meeting point is at my house. I leave the kite with Doug on my front porch and I run to my room, where I have my kite string drawer. I have several different thicknesses and lengths of string and several balls of string. I grab them all. When I get back outside, Doug is standing in the breeze with my kite fully assembled in his hand. What a fine kite it is. No one is there except Doug and me.

He tells me, "Go inside and ask your mom for some old bed sheets so we can make a tail." Off I go to the basement where my mom is doing laundry. When I ask for old bed sheets for the tail of the kite my mom points to the hamper under the stairs where she keeps old clothes, towels, and sheets. Under the stairs is Calico's domain, so I tread lightly. I grab an old blue sheet and race up to the front porch. By this time George and Skip are back with handfuls of string. What a grand day so far. It gets a lot better.

Doug takes out his pocket knife, the one with the pearl handle, and cuts the sheet into strips about two inches wide and as wide as the sheet, maybe five feet. These will make a glorious tail. Now Doug shows us how to attach the kite string to the string yoke on the kite, so that the kite will not be too upright or too flat when it flies. This appears to be somewhat scientific and we are listening intently to the master. Finally, the first section of string is attached to the kite. The tail, made of three lengths of blue sheet, is attached by a knot to the string perimeter and the bottom wood support.

We walk across Foster to set up at the edge of the asphalt parking lot of the new shopping center. In seconds the kite is in the air about ten feet off the ground, Doug is letting out string like crazy, and the kite is rising up into the blustery blue sky, climbing ever higher above the southwest wind. It is very windy, with strong gusts. The first length of string has been let all of the way out, maybe one hundred feet. The kite rocks back and forth with the edges flapping in the breeze. When we get near the end of the first ball of string, Doug is holding on to the end of the string which he has wrapped around a stick he brought along for the occasion.

Now he is calling for more string, from the balls we each brought with us. He takes the second ball of string from George. While I hold the stick, which takes a lot of strength, he ties the new string to the old string loop, which is around the stick, and slowly removes the stick. He is holding the second ball of string and letting out line quickly. How he knows how to do this is a mystery. Somehow, he knows exactly what to do. We are all amazed. Again, Doug is our hero. Higher and higher the wind raises the bright yellow kite with the light blue tail up into the deep blue sky.

It is now mid-afternoon, with the sun dropping lower in the sky and the wind still howling, even stronger than earlier in the day. We have added five balls of string and now have to add more tail to the kite. Doug holds the kite stick at the end of the string, while Skipper, who is the tallest of us, excepting Doug, runs toward the kite with the string under his arm, through the parking lot. When he gets to the kite he pulls it down to ground level. He ties on two lengths, or about ten feet of tail. According to Doug the more wind and height of the kite the more tail it needs.

Doug gives Skip a wave to let him release the kite with its enormous tail. Before Skip left to add more tail, Doug told him not to touch the tail when he let go of the kite. As he lets go of the string, he is way out in the parking lot. Skip is careful not to touch the tail as he lets go of the kite. The little kite soars up into the sky. It is much more stable now in the ever-increasing winds because of the added tail length. After over an hour we have added another four balls of string, which has let the kite rise up so high that it is a small yellow speck in the sky. That is all the string we have. The wind is now blowing even harder as the sun is going down. We are settling down to enjoy our high-flying kite with the longest string in the world.

Then it happens.

George is holding the end of the string tied to the stick. We hear nothing except George saying, "Uh, oh," and see nothing except the string go limp on his end.

Doug shouts, "Everybody watch the kite. See where it's going."

The kite wiggles side to side as it falls silently down, down, down. We all watch to see where it might land but our vision is blocked by the trees to the north of the construction site. Lye's neighborhood.

Doug shouts again, "Guys, let's go get it before Lye and his gang do." It is a call to arms. George immediately drops the stick and the limp string and we all start running across the parking lot toward where the kite appeared to be going when it was falling. Doug is concerned it went across Harlem Avenue to the east. I am afraid Lye will get to the kite first. After all, it is my kite.

The sun is now close to setting when we get to the east side of Lye's neighborhood, along Harlem Avenue. It is not hard to track down the kite. We are following the string. It crosses Harlem about where my family's dentist office is located several blocks north of Foster. The string lays on the pavement with cars running over it. Then it climbs up a tree near the intersection of Farragut Avenue. The kite is in full view in an elm tree as we are dodging traffic to get across Harlem Avenue.

There it is, hanging by ten feet of string from a lower branch of the tree between the curb and the sidewalk, swaying in the wind. We are fortunate that it is near the ground and that the kite is not damaged in any way. That was a close one. Doug boosts up George. Reaching up as far as he can, George pulls the kite by the string gently out of the tree. He gives it to me for safe keeping as we all follow Doug back across busy Harlem Avenue, taking the run-over string in the street with us.

When we get back to the launch site near Foster across the street from my house, Doug coils up what is left of the string into a huge ball that requires several sticks to contain it all. We have a good laugh about the length of string we used. We also have another laugh about the long, long tail on the kite. We have a laugh about the fun we had. Finally, I give thanks to God that Lye did not get my kite.

CHAPTER SEVEN

THE REFRIGERATOR
AND THE BUG SPRAY TRUCK

It is a warm, muggy Sunday afternoon in the summer of 1959. After coming home from church, I want to ride my bike. As I am passing through the living room I look outside to see if any of my friends are down at my end of the block. Sadly, there is nobody there. I still want to see if anybody wants to ride bikes so when I find my mom in the kitchen I tell her, "Mom I would like to ride my bike today. I'm going over to Skip's house."

Mom says, "OK. Let us know where you are going if you leave the neighborhood."

"I will," I say. I climb the stair to my bedroom and change clothes.

I get my bike, the red-and-chrome Schwinn, out of the garage and slowly ride on the sidewalk past the Flynn's house, over to Skip's house, two houses to the west on Foster Avenue. I am at his back door.

"Yo, Skip, let's ride," I shout.

Skip's mom comes to the window overlooking the Flynn's driveway and says, "He will be out in a minute. How are you, Johnny?"

"Fine, Mrs. Mac Murray," I say. So I wait. As I am standing with my bike between my legs, Donna, Skip's sister, looks out the window at me and smiles, then disappears into the kitchen.

As I am waiting, I daydream about the house between Skip's and my house, owned by the Flynns. The kids in the Oconto Gang fear the Flynns. We fear them like we fear the devil. They never talk to us kids except to tell us to stay out of their yard. One day while throwing pitches with tennis balls against my garage door, in training, I imagine, for the Cubs, one of the tennis balls bounced off the sidewalk, headed for the hedge in my back yard and, like it had eyes, landed in the Flynn's back yard. The coast looked clear so I crawled under the high hedge that separated my yard from the Flynn's yard to retrieve the ball. As I reached for the yellow ball Mr. Flynn rounded the corner of his house and saw me. He could feel my fear. He just stood there.

I was most frightened, and with a rapidly beating heart said, "Just getting my ball, sir." He continued to stand there, not saying a word. I crawled back under the hedge to safety.

It is several minutes before Skip emerges from his house, which brings me back to the present, and appears on his back porch, ready to ride. We walk with a bounce in our step to his garage and get out his bike, a dark-blue Schwinn with a book rack on back. Just as we are discussing where we are to ride, George shows up on his bike, a brown-and-white Schwinn.

Then George says, "Hey, look at that old refrigerator over there."

This old appliance has seen better days. It is sitting next to some household junk ready for the garbage man, behind the Flynn's back porch, which is in view of the north side of Skipper's house that leads to his back porch. The old refrigerator is white with a slightly rounded top, and the door has been removed for some reason. We do not see the door anywhere. But that does not matter to us kids since we are intrigued. For us twelve-year-olds, it makes a terrific fort and a hiding place.

George says, as the instigator, "Who wants to try it out?"

We all look at each other and I say, "I will." I get down on my hands and knees and creep under the fridge as Skip and George lower it over my entire body. At first I am thinking this is really cool and makes a great hiding place. There is plenty of room for two of us guys in here. Then Skip and George lower the fridge some more. As they lower it even more to about two feet off the ground, I hear, "I can't hold it," and, "Neither can I."

Then the open end of the fridge wobbles and crashes to the ground with an earth-shaking thud. I am suddenly panicked. All is dark except a thin stream of light coming in where the fridge now barely touches the ground all around me. I scream, "Get me out of here, you guys. I'm scared." I hear nothing. Several seconds pass.

Then Skip says, "It's too heavy. We can't lift it up. We dropped it."

"Let's get Doug," shouts George. I hear them faintly, since I am trapped under a heavy fridge, riding away, which does not make me feel any better. However, it makes me feel better that they are going to get Doug. I am praying that this works out, without adults knowing about it, and that Doug can lift this thing up and off me before I suffocate.

I cry out loud since time is dragging on. Nobody comes to get me out of this inverted prison. It is very dark with only that sliver of light coming in at the ground. After a while, I do not know how long, I am pounding on the sides of the fridge. Several minutes later my pounding gets slower due to the pain in my hands. Just after I stop my pounding, I hear the voices of Doug, Skip, and George. Doug is saying to spread out and get around the fridge on all three sides to get better leverage. I then see the wiggling fingers of my friends poking under the edges of the fridge at the ground. Then the fridge begins to tip from side to side, move upward slowly at first, and then a little higher for me to wiggle my body out along the ground. I am feeling better but still anxious. As my feet clear the end of the fridge, Doug, Skip, and George drop it to the ground. I lie on the ground looking at Skip's house and start to cry.

Doug kneels down next to me, puts his hand on my head and says, "JT, you're OK now." Even though I am shaking from head to toe, I am fine because of Doug.

At this point, I say, "I need to go home, fellas."

To which Doug replies, "I understand. Let him go, guys."

Without looking at anybody, I get on my bike and ride home. I avoid seeing my parents or Juil. I go straight to my room, take off my shoes, and lie down in the comfort of my bed to take a nap.

After a while, my mom wakes me up.

I react quickly with, "What time is it, Mom?"

"Oh, about six o'clock. Ready for dinner soon."

I am still in a slight fog from just waking up, but in spite of my feeling foggy I hear the guys outside on their bikes. I make sure I am composed, get my shoes on, and slink out of the house. The sun is going down, but the bug spray truck will be coming around since it is Sunday evening.

We usually wait down near my house for the bug spray truck. It comes from the east on Foster then turns sharply left at Oconto in front of my house. The truck is a weird-looking vehicle. The front looks normal for a pick-up style truck, but in the location of the bed are a huge tank, platform, and nozzle on both sides to spray the fog on both sides of the vehicle as it moves forward.

As I join the group, Skip, George, and Doug on his racing bike with the small tires are circling in the street by my driveway. They are also turning up the driveway and riding on the sidewalk. They all give me a wave as we pass each other in the circling pattern. I feel so good that I ride south on Oconto down the sidewalk very fast past Doug's house, cutting across George's driveway into the street and then back north on Oconto.

As I am reaching my driveway we all hear the motor-like sound of the bug spray truck coming west on Foster Avenue. It is blowing lots of fog as its turn-signal blinks on and off and the front wheels turn toward the entrance to Oconto. What great timing. The four of us gather in front of my driveway to wait for the truck to pass us by, and then with Doug in the lead, we pedal as fast as we can to catch up with the truck and its foggy trail. The most fun is riding in the fog near the gutter on each side of the street and not being able to see too much, like an airplane in the clouds.

In the cool late afternoon air we pass Carmen Avenue and follow the loud smoking monster as it continues south on Oconto. Soon we are at the end of Oconto. It is time to turn around and head home as the truck turns west on West Ainslie Street. The day has had its ups and downs, from being buried alive under a refrigerator to flying in the clouds on my bike. It sure has been interesting.

Doug circles around in the street to point us back toward home. As the bug spray fog is dwindling away, encroaching on the houses on each side of the street, we follow Doug back to our block with smiles on our faces. If it were not for him I might still be under that darn refrigerator. If not for him we would not have been flying in the clouds behind the bug spray truck. Most importantly, because of him my parents or any other adult knows nothing of the refrigerator adventure that could have killed me. Even so I am suspicious of a group of adults at the end of our block talking with each other. I am hoping they are talking about those foolish kids riding their bikes through the bug spray fog and not about the kid that got caught under the refrigerator.

I put my bike in the garage on its kick stand and carefully close the garage door so it does not slam shut. As I sit down to dinner with my family, I feel very fortunate to be there. I survived the killer refrigerator so I could ride in the clouds. Thanks, Doug.

CHAPTER EIGHT

BIKE RIDE

In the springtime of 1961 on a Saturday, the Oconto Gang did a marvelous thing. We rode our bikes under the guidance of Doug from little old Oconto Avenue to The Naval Air Station in Glenview, Illinois. It was a time before our gang would be splintered into different high schools and Doug would be in military service and out of the area.

At about six-thirty my dad offers to make pancakes for breakfast, but in order not to delay the start of the trip, I say no and instead have a bowl of cereal with milk, and orange juice. I see out of the kitchen window over the sink that Doug is the first to arrive on his Gitane racing bike, with the skinny, high-pressure tires. It has the kind of handle bars that curl back so one can lean way forward while pedaling at high speed. It is the kind of bike that I want to have when I am his age.

Doug's plan for the day starts with each of us checking our bikes out in my garage. The checklist includes tire-pressure check and tightness of handlebar clamps as well as lubrication of the chain, and a battery-check for our head-lights. I hear Skip talking with Doug and George. The tire pump and oil can I left in the garage are available for their use and they waste no time using them. My mom gives me a bag of sandwiches she made last night for us kids to have for lunch. I put them in my saddlebags for later. Doug reminds us to take some money and drink water before we leave. He and I have water-bottle holders on our bikes. He asks me to fill up both his and my bottle with water from the hose bibb on my garage. I fill up our plastic bottles and all of us get a long drink of water. It is about seven o'clock now and Doug is making sure everybody is ready both physically and mentally. He is chatting with each of us to get our minds going. We all are really looking forward to this ride, so there is no negative talk or whining. Even though it is early George is not whining. He really looks ready. The time is nigh. Doug steps onto his bike, the rest of us do the same and we are out on Oconto in a flash.

We cross Foster at Oconto to ride on the sidewalk on the north side of Foster to avoid the traffic light at Harlem. As we ride north on Harlem at Farragut, Doug reminds us that we are now in Lye's territory, so look alive and stare straight ahead. We continue north to Higgins where we stop at the traffic light. I look to my right to see Dr. Lally's office where my mom takes me for medical care.

Dr. Lally also makes house calls. He is a very decent man and helped me especially when I broke my arm playing baseball. I caught a fly ball as the right fielder, but the second baseman tried to get the ball out of my hand. I would not let go of the ball, so he broke my lower arm trying to pry it out of my hand.

Next we ride across Talcott, where Immaculate Conception School and Church are located. George's sister goes to school there and George will probably go there to school as well. Also on Talcott is Resurrection Hospital, where my mom went for a hernia operation. We are now getting quite far from home, crossing the big busy intersections of Avondale, Northwest Highway, and Devon.

For the next several minutes we are looking at homes on the left and a very large cemetery on our right as we enter into the community of Niles at Touhy Avenue. We all sense that we are very far away from our block and our families. We also sense that we are safe because of Doug's presence and leadership. We cross Milwaukee Avenue, Oakton, and then Dempster. We are really far from home now. I am feeling a bit lonely and uneasy. However, we all know Glenview and its Navy jets flying over our heads is just around the corner.

At the intersection of Dempster and Harlem we take a long-needed break. While the temperature is bearable the humidity is high. We are tired and sweating through our shirts. It is a residential neighborhood with many older trees. One particularly large elm tree offers us its shade. Doug and I break out our water bottles and everyone shares in soothing their dry throats with fresh water.

Doug takes a map from his pocket as we watch him look intensely at the map and say, "We are right on track, guys." We say nothing.

In ten minutes Doug says, "Let's pack up and go. Do you guys want to see those jets?"

We all yell out, "Yeah!"

We take our bikes off their kick stands, throw our legs over the top bar, and gladly follow Doug to the jets.

We continue our northern trek on Harlem Avenue through the residential community until we get to Milwaukee Avenue. It is a big intersection with Mayhill Catholic Cemetery on the southwest corner. I had been to a funeral there with my family a while ago. We pass Ballard Road. I feel like I am in an area that I know, but I really do not know exactly where I am. My Aunt Florence and Uncle Jack have a very nice home off of Ballard Road. Then we cross Maryland Street. We arrive at a major development called Golf Mill Shopping Center, a huge retail mall, just recently completed. We pass another cemetery called Ridgewood Memorial. I have never been to this cemetery. Our gang of energetic souls cheerfully pedals on.

Now we are passing through the forest preserve that borders the Des Plaines River. My dad had just told me the other day that the forest preserve is dedicated land and woods set aside by the City of Chicago for the enjoyment of the public and that it will never be built upon. We are riding through the woods on Milwaukee Road, Route 21 as we merge with River Road, Route 45. We cross over the Des Plaines River. My dad's older brother Al and his family live on River Road, with the east end of their property backing up to the Des Plaines River. My dad and I had been catfishing on Uncle Al's dock several times. I remember the river being very swift and a muddy brown color. I think their property is near Euclid, which is far south of where our bike group is traveling. There is good news. At our present location we can hear the Navy jets at the NAS Glenview. The sound of them makes us pedal faster. It is like a whistle to a dog. We get on Lake Avenue and head east.

When we get to the airfield, in front of us is a high chain-link fence with barbed wire that runs parallel to the main runway to provide security for this government installation. We get to the corner of the fence to witness a Navy fighter taking off right in front of us. We all look at each other, eyes and mouths wide open. George is jumping up and down.

Doug says, "Let's camp out across the road and have our lunch that Mrs. Snell made. I'm really hungry. How about you guys?"

We all shout, "Yeah."

Following his lead, we cross the highway carefully to get to the other side. Since there are some wooded areas located on the east side of the road, we find a comfortable spot to park our bikes, sit down, and enjoy eating lunch. I break out the homemade sandwiches from my saddlebag. It does not get any better than this. Another dark blue jet takes off while we are eating. It is very loud. Over the roar of the aircraft Doug says it is either a Skyhawk or a Panther, or maybe it is a Banshee. We all look at Doug with admiration, since he knows the types of Navy aircraft taking off in front of us.

"One day I would like to be a pilot," I say to myself. I imagine we all feel that way today. As we are eating lunch, I daydream about when I was very young, maybe six or seven. My parents and Aunt Myrtle took me to see Santa Claus at NAS Glenview. What a special treat. I remember being seated on Santa Claus' knee after he came out of a DC-3 aircraft that landed at NAS Glenview and slowly taxied over to where we were waiting near the tower. Of all the kids there to welcome Santa he picked me to sit on his lap for a photograph. I was a bit frightened but held out until Santa gently put me down and my Aunt Myrtle held me tight in her arms. I was to find out many years later that Santa was my Uncle John's father.

Doug looks at his watch, studies the map for a few seconds, looks at us kids and says, "OK, gang, let's go!"

It is about three o'clock in the afternoon when we turn right on Foster off of Harlem. The ride home is a continuous fast ride with no stops of any kind. We are so pumped up that we feel we are Navy aviators on a mission of life and death. We all have our game faces on since we have just accomplished a feat none of us thought we could do. We are moving very fast over the ground, but imagine we are aircraft in formation in the sky. As I arrive at my house I turn in at my driveway and give a thumbs up to everybody else headed home to their houses. I lift up the garage door and park my bike inside next to my dad's 1958 Chevy Bel Air.

As I enter my house my mom asks, "How was the bike trip?"

I say, "It was neat."

Without hesitation she says, "Go upstairs and take a shower, Sergeant," with a smile on her face.

My dad is there too to see me come home, which is a rare occurrence on a Saturday, since he usually works at the lumber yard on Saturdays. He smiles too and pats me on the head. I am sure both of them are happy to see me arrive home and in one piece. I feel glad to be home.

Only Doug could have made this special day happen. This day was all good.

CHAPTER NINE

THE MAGNIFICENT BUILDING

oug has recently graduated from Maine East High School, and when I see him I notice he looks much older. After all, he is about four years older than me. I am getting older too. Since I do not have an older brother, I am learning to watch Doug for signs of what my life may be like in four years. It is a Saturday in the early summer of 1961. I have just graduated from Pennoyer School, an elementary school, and will be entering Luther North High School in the fall. Skip and George will be going to a Catholic high school.

There was a storm last night, but today the weather has changed, and it looks like it will be a fine day. Unfortunately, this beautiful Saturday morning I am having only a big bowl of cereal with milk. No pancakes. My dad is working at the lumber yard early today. I am proud of my dad. He has recently taken this job to bring in some additional income. He likes working at the lumber yard. During the week he sells construction equipment for a local construction supply company. My mom, who used to be a stay at home mom, now works weekdays at a local high school as a secretary. At about nine o'clock there is a knock on the front door. I carry my bowl and spoon to the front door. Doug is there with his sketch-pad case in one hand and a small case of drawing pencils in the other. I ask him to come in. Mom shouts from the basement, "Who is it, Johnny?"

I reply, "It's Doug."

Doug asks me if I want to go on a field trip to do some drawing. He has gotten permission to use his Dad's car. I feel like this will be fun, because I have been doing some sketching for a little newspaper I have been making and passing out on the school bus every week or so. I tell him this sounds good to me. While in the basement, I tell Mom that Doug asked me to go on a field trip to do some sketching.

She says, "Johnny, I do not worry when you are out with Dougie. He is a good friend. I trust him. Go and have a good time."

Nothing like getting a vote of confidence from my mom. I get my drawing paper and pencils, erasers, and a straight edge from my work table in the basement. Also, at the last minute I take a pre-made hard canvas board, which is about eight inches by ten inches. It fits snugly into my drawing case along with my sketch paper and other materials. I had seen on TV that some artists use canvas boards under their drawing paper to give a nice texture to a pencil drawing. I had done some experimentation at home and liked the results in my school bus newspaper. I grab one for Doug too.

Doug has parked the Dodge Coronet in front of our house facing north, on the left side of the street. *How odd*, I thought, but he probably did not want to park across the street. Anyway, I get in the car riding shotgun. I have no idea where we are going.

Then Doug says, "We are going to a special place. Have you been to Bahi'a Temple?"

I shake my head no.

"You'll like it, JT."

I have a feeling of euphoria. I will be with Doug in his car going on a field trip on a beautiful Saturday to a place that Doug likes a lot and I have never seen before. A one-on-one with Doug. It does not get much better than this. I have never been in his dad's car. While I am looking around at the dashboard and other neat stuff, I notice the way he is sitting in the driver's seat with his left elbow out the open window, and his right wrist huddling over the top of the steering wheel, with a slightly slouching posture.

I kind of recognize the area we are driving through since my folks told me they used to hang out as teens around the Irving Park and Damen area. They have driven through this area with my sister and me several times before, showing us their old stomping grounds. We pass Winnemac Park driving into the morning sun on Foster. I put my sun shade down. Doug puts his down too. We are now on Clark Street after turning left from the long drive on Foster. We are driving through the great North Side neighborhoods of Chicago. Then we are crossing Devon Avenue. When we are passing Calvary Cemetery, Doug speaks.

He blurts out, "I have joined the Air Force, JT." He pauses. He looks apprehensive. "Don't worry. I'll be OK. What do you think?"

My heart shatters from this news. I get a one-on-one with Doug and he drops a bomb like this. With a stiff upper lip, I respond coolly, "Sounds OK to me, Doug. Will you be around Chicago?" thinking of Rantoul Air Force Base in Southern Illinois.

"I don't know where they will send me, but I leave for basic training soon."

Good Grief. This day has turned into a complete disaster. How much more can a fourteen-year-old boy take? We drive on, going north, and get onto Sheridan Road. We pass Northwestern University positioned near the shore of Lake Michigan. Peter, one of the assistant scoutmasters in my Boy Scout Troop, is enrolled in the music program there. I am looking out the side window trying to hold back tears. I look at Doug. Doug has grown up. He will be far, far away and may never return. I am losing a good friend. I have grown up too. This means we are not going to play the same games as when we were young.

On the other hand, Doug is doing his part to contribute to a civil society by joining the Air Force. Perhaps he is expecting me to follow his lead. I am thinking about how I can contribute to this civil society as well.

As I am looking at the passing scenery, I am taken away from my grief by noticing that the homes and properties in this area are nothing short of spectacular. Block after block of beautiful homes surrounded by old stately trees and well-tended lawns. We are in Wilmette. It is nothing like Harwood Heights.

Doug knows I am upset, but besides being upset, I understand he had to tell me his plans, because we are friends. I do understand. The farther we drive north into the beautiful neighborhoods of Wilmette the better I feel. The experience is therapeutic to me and Doug is smiling. He's pointing out homes that he wants to live in when he returns from his service with the Air Force.

"It won't be that long, JT. I'll be back before you know it."

I respond, "Yeah, you're right, Doug. I hope you own a house here someday."

Then, I see a magnificent building just above the gracious trees that line Sheridan Road. It is the Baha'i Temple. It is captivating. I forget about Doug, the Air Force, and crying inside. This is what he wants me to see. I will never forget the view and the moment—an enormous white house of God with its roof pointing toward heaven.

As I am getting excited, I ask myself where we are going to set up to make some drawings. I am sure Doug knows a good spot. In fact, he does, as he heads the Coronet down the west side of the beautiful building to its private parking lot along the river. I cannot take my eyes from the architectural detail of the building and its ornately landscaped grounds. We are both focused now.

Doug asks, "What do you think; is this great or what?" Little does he know what a fabulous treat this is for me.

I say, "This is great, Doug."

He pulls into an open spot in the parking lot on the west side of the property. We look around and find a place in the shade on a concrete retaining wall to set up. Doug gets out his drawing paper and pencils, finds his place at the end of the retaining wall, and quickly starts to sketch the massive pointed top of the building before him. I, on the other end of the wall, orient myself toward the river turning to face west and catch sight of a small sloop on anchor nearby in the Sheridan Yacht Club. I think about the sailboat that Doug's brother is still building in the driveway of Doug's house. It kind of looks the same. I think that making a drawing of a sailboat will be appropriate, but I know it will be challenging because I have not worked on such a complex project before. I need this challenge. Also, I feel this is Doug's outing. He planned it and he deserves to draw the temple.

Even though the weather and the scenery are perfect, initially, I am having trouble with my sketch of the sailboat even with the textured canvas under my sketch paper. After about fifteen minutes, Doug comes over to observe how I am doing. He sees I am floundering, with three sheets of paper started but little to show for my effort thus far. He sees I need some encouragement.

As he gets closer, my thoughts are still on his leaving for the Air Force.

He says, "JT, don't think about me going into the Air Force. Think about the sailboat over there that you are sketching. See that none of its surfaces are straight. They are all curved. If you think about it that way, you will get it. Come on, JT. I am counting on you to become a great architect when you grow up. You can do this. Just remember: no straight lines. All of its surfaces are curved."

I just look at him. I really needed that.

Doug goes back to his perch on the other end of the concrete wall. I notice he is using the pre-made hard canvas board I gave him. I return to my work, renewed by selecting a new sheet of paper to begin sketching the sailboat with a pencil that I just sharpened. I start with the gunwale, drawing a curved line that sets the scale of the 20 foot long boat, and positions the boat properly in the water. It is the easiest line to draw. It is gently curved.

Next, the water line. I carefully shade the lower parts of the hull and the reflection of the glossy hull in the water. Then on to the deck, windows, hatch, mast, boom, and rails. The pieces are fitting together as I slowly create a picture of the sailboat located not more than twenty feet in front of me. The wind blows up, the air smells fresh, and with Doug's mentoring I am turning my sadness into creative artwork and the results are pretty good. As I am finishing up my pencil sketch the boat comes alive from a wind gust, changing its position and rocking slightly side to side.

I have been working now maybe an hour or so on my creation which is virtually complete, have come to a breaking point, and now want to see Doug's drawing of the magnificent building. As I approach him from behind, he does not flinch, even though he is in deep concentration.

Without looking at me he asks, "Do you want to see it?"

I am looking over his shoulder while he is putting the finishing touches on his sketch. I think his sketch is as magnificent as the building, with all the details, arched buttresses, and the surrounding trees and other vegetation.

"I am just finishing up. Give me a little more time, OK?"

"OK, Doug" I say quietly. I ask him for a blue colored pencil since the hull of the boat that I have drawn has a blue hull from the water-line to the gunwale. Doug, now deeper in thought and wanting to finish up, casually motions to his box of pencils.

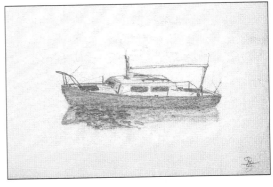

After finding one that is the right color to match the boat, I go back to my position and lightly fill in the hull with the blue color. The color is perfect. My drawing is complete. As I reflect on the day, I did struggle some in the beginning but with Doug's help I have created a stunning work of art.

As I am packing up my small drawing supply case and carefully putting my drawing into it to make sure it does not get torn or even wrinkled, Doug is also packing up. He asks me if he can look at my drawing of the sailboat. I pull it out of my artist case and show it to him.

He says, "Now that is a good drawing." He then shows me his finished sketch of the Baha'i House of Worship. It is beautiful. Doug is a most talented artist.

It is a long ride home. It is early afternoon. Having spent the whole morning away from home and being out in the fresh air we both are really hungry. We stop at the Dairy Queen on Lake Avenue for hamburgers and milkshakes. Doug pays. We eat while Doug is driving, and we have a lot of fun telling stories. I notice we are back on Foster Avenue near Central. I will be changing buses here when I go off to high school at Luther North. I will be changing from the Foster bus to the Central bus each morning. In the evening, I will change from the Central bus to the Foster bus.

The big Dodge pulls us up the slight hill as we head toward Harlem Avenue and our home turf on the Oconto block. When he drops me off at my house it is a bittersweet parting. The day has been one of the high points in my life, but I do not know if I will see Doug again. He said he is going away soon. When is that? I try not to think about Doug going away. I am feeling a lot older and a lot more accomplished as an artist for a fourteen-year-old boy.

As I am leaving the car he says, "Take care, JT," and I say, "Thanks for everything, Doug."

We both look at each other for a second or two knowing we may not see each other again for a long time if ever again. We are both growing older and are on our way to becoming adults. As adults I know we will be going our separate ways. It is a natural part of life. Then he does an amazing thing. He reaches into the back seat, grabs his drawing case, and lays it on his lap. He then carefully opens it up and gives me his pencil drawing of the magnificent building. But before he hands it to me, he tears out and keeps the small section at the bottom with his initials on it. I am crying inside again. I am thinking that he is afraid of dying while in the Air Force and wants his drawing to live on with me, through me, and in me. Or he may just be keeping the torn-out piece with his initials as memorabilia of this fine day with his friend JT.

He says, "You take this drawing …for safe keeping, JT."

As you can see, I did.

CHAPTER TEN

DOUG'S LETTER

I am fifteen years old. One day in April I receive a letter in the mail. My mom gives the envelope to me after breakfast, saying, "Looks like a letter from Dougie for you, Johnny."

Mom is right. It is postmarked from the state of Washington and has Doug's name and address at an Air Force Base written in the upper left corner. Now I am truly excited. I find my space in the dining room on the carpeted floor, up against the window that looks out over the front yard. It is the window I like to stare out of when I am day dreaming. I carefully open the slightly wrinkled envelope and read.

> Hey JT,
>
> Here I am in the great northwest. I am stationed at McChord Air Force Base, Tacoma, Washington. They encourage us to write letters to stay in touch with our friends and relatives so as to not lose sight of who we are fighting for. I made it through basic training with flying colors, since I was in pretty good shape from exercising and running around the block prior to leaving for the Air Force.
>
> How is everything with you? Are you doing well at Luther North High School? I hope so. Do not let us down. You are a smart kid and will do well in anything that you put your mind to. Hey, you would make an excellent architect.
>
> Here we are flying missions to rescue people mostly in boats in the Pacific and in Puget Sound. We have a helicopter

and several airmen that man the helicopter in our rescue operations. I am one of the airmen. It is very interesting and sometimes dangerous depending on the weather.

Before I go I wanted to tell you that we are being told that the relations between the Soviet Union and the USA are tense in the cold war as they call it. Even in the Bible there is a reference that the Eagle and the Bear will fight. So it may be true that we will end up in some kind of conflict. I do not know.

Please take care of yourself and give my regards to your whole family. I really miss being back on the block with my friends, including you.

See you soon,
Doug

PS: This country was founded on exercising God's Law in our daily life, including the structure of the government set forth in the Declaration of Independence and the Constitution.

Our society if you can call it that has abandoned God's Law in favor of man's law, with all of the imperfections that go along with it. Our society has degenerated and continues to degenerate. Ultimately, the settlement will come to "my way or your way" which will require confrontation to address the differences.

Our society cannot tolerate terrorism. Good people must stand for God's law which may require standing up and fighting literally for what is right.

As I finish reading the letter and stare out the window, I remember how Doug always exhibited concern for others, sometimes over concern for himself. Now here he is in the Air Force, risking his life to help other people in need. I see him now not just as a friend and mentor, but as a patriot. He is dedicating his life, and may give his life, in defense of our country.

Years from now as a father, I will tell my children the stories that are written in this book. I will become an architect, as he suggested to me at the magnificent building. I will enlist in the US Army after finishing college.

I believe Doug realizes that we are very much alike. In his letter he encourages me to face the unknown just like he is facing the unknown. He shares with me the experiences of life. He shares them with me to shape me into a better person. He wants me to use my God-given artistic talents for good. He has the same talents, but wants me to put them to better use.

While reading that letter, I realize I am truly blessed to have Doug as my friend.

Still sitting at my favorite window, I am observing that the grass in my yard is green and the sky above is blue. A car goes slowly by my house, north on Oconto, stops at the stop sign, and turns right on Foster Avenue. I feel like an era of my life has just ended and an entirely new era is coming. It is 1961.

CHAPTER ELEVEN

THE BLUE BIKE AND THE BLACK BUG

It is the fall of 1966, and a chilly day, as I get off the Chicago Transit Authority bus on Foster Avenue across the street from my house. After I take the subway to Logan Square from the University of Illinois Circle Campus where I am attending college, I take two separate buses to get home: the Milwaukee Avenue bus and then the Foster Avenue bus. This day, Doug's father is the bus driver on the Foster bus, so he lets me off directly across Foster from my house instead of at the prescribed bus stop on Harlem Avenue.

He says, "Have a good day, Johnny. Say hello to your mom and dad for me."

I say, "Thanks, Mr. Lind. I will."

I quickly exit the bus with my black leather briefcase given to me by my Aunt Myrtle. It is heavy with books and other materials, since I have lots of homework. I have a drawing table with a small light above it set up in my bedroom where I do my work. It is a little tight but works for me.

Some days I like to ride the bus and other days I don't. After all, I had been riding the bus every day to and from Luther North High School for the previous four years. I had gotten my fill of bus riding. Now that I am older and have been working part time at the local doughnut shop, Alvin's Donuts, with my friend Fred, I have been able to put together some money in my savings account at the Savings and Loan on Harlem. Quite surprisingly, I have saved maybe $2,000.

Several months ago, I had been at my grandfather's house in Elmwood Park and got the great opportunity to ride a small Honda 50cc motorcycle owned by the son of his neighbor. I actually laid it down, but it was fun to ride it and, luckily, I laid it down on the grass, not the pavement. It was then that I decided to buy a motorcycle.

It is a glorious Saturday. I ride the CTA to Midwest Triumph in Chicago. I take the Foster bus to the Cicero bus. While riding the bus I feel like this is going to be my last bus trip. What I am really seeking is freedom, although I am not consciously aware of it. I am also a little scared of making the purchase and riding it home. It was good fortune that I rode the small Honda 50cc machine at my grandfather's. It was several months before, but I remember the feel of it. When I arrive at Midwest Triumph it is just opening time. A fellow with a buzz cut of blond hair, maybe thirty years old, wearing a Midwest Triumph T-shirt and jeans opens the front door.

He says, "Welcome to Midwest Triumph. My name is William. What's yours?"

I say, "My name is John, and I am looking for a motorcycle, sir."

"New or used?" he responds.

"I think used." I had already noticed the prices of the new bikes by the front windows. In the back of the store there are several really good-looking used bikes for sale. I like one with a chrome tank and a luggage rack, but it is $500, which is more than the $400 cash in my pocket. Right next to it is a pretty one with a blue and white tank and white fenders with a blue stripe down the middle. I do not see any dents or scratches. When I look at the price tag it is $450. Very disappointing. At eighteen years old, I kind of feel like walking out but I think to myself, what would Doug do? William wants to sell me a motorcycle. Looking him straight in the eye, I say to William, who told me later he was the owner, that I only have $400.

He hesitates slightly but then says, "That's a deal. Four hundred, out the door."

The exchange of money and paperwork is minimal. With my mind spinning around, after he has his mechanic check the compression, put in a new set of spark plugs, and fill the gas tank, I am kick-starting the machine near the back garage door to the alley. After two solid kicks she begins to purr. Then I ride all the way home, smiling and making great sounds with my "new" 1964 650cc Triumph. I remind myself that I need to get my motorcycle certification.

When I get home my dad is at work and my mom does not notice, since she is studying for a course she is taking at Roosevelt University in the education program. She hopes to eventually graduate and become a teacher in the Chicago Public School System.

By the following Saturday, I finally get everything taken care of, including insurance, to be certified as an operator of a motorcycle. This is truly a momentous day in my life.

Several weeks later, it is a cool Saturday in early October. My mom does not like the motorcycle, while my dad thinks it is cool. He is of British lineage and thinks my purchase of a Triumph is a good choice. He even gives me a few bucks to help out initially. Doug, Skip, and George all think it is boss. I like its mellow-sounding pipes, its distinctive blue color with white trim, and its speedometer and tachometer. I love my motorcycle.

Even so, I do not ride the bike today because the temperature is expected to be in the 50s, which is a challenge to the senses when riding a motorcycle. I had learned my lesson on my first ride to and from school last week, when the temperature was fine in the morning but dipped down to the low 40s in late afternoon, when I left school. After all, this is Chicago in the fall, when the weather is sometimes unpredictable. On my ride home my fingers were numb and frozen around the hand grips when I got off the Kennedy Expressway at Harlem. Ouch. When I got home and parked the bike in the garage, the first thing I did was take a hot shower. But this evening something will happen that is quite unexpected and wonderful.

It is after dinner. I beg off watching TV because I have a load of homework for Algebra and for my design class, where I am making a line drawing in black ink of the newly constructed Chicago Civic Center in downtown Chicago. I climb the stairs to the second floor and enter my room, switching on the light as I sit down at my work table. I am just about finished with the Algebra homework, checking the answers in the back of the book, when the doorbell rings. I kind of ignore it because I am still in homework mode.

After some time, Dad calls to me, "Hey, Johnny, Doug is here to see you."

I think a visit from Doug on this Saturday night is odd. I walk downstairs to the living room to see him standing there smiling near the front door. He and my dad are looking at each other as they talk. Doug looks over at me.

"Johnny, I am selling my wife's black Beetle. Would you like to buy it?"

Doug explains that he is working at the O'Hare airport as ground crew and Carol is working at the Pure Oil Company. You see, he and his new wife Carol are living in his parents' house temporarily now that he is back from the Air

Force. Doug served his time and came home from the Air Force in 1964. They were married on May 1, 1965.

My dad stands there looking at me too. It seems like they have cooked up something in advance, but I go along anyway.

I say, "Wow. Why are you selling it?"

Doug says his wife needs a vehicle with an automatic transmission, and the Beetle has a stick shift. As he says this, my mind remembers that last week, as I was getting up to go to school early in the morning, I heard a car on Foster Avenue grinding its gears while shifting as it sped west in the dark. Maybe this was Doug's wife, Carol.

Anyway, after his explanation I say, "I would be pleased to buy your wife's bug. How much are you asking?"

He says, "$800."

My dad says, "That is a good price, money bags."

He is looking at me. He refers to me as money bags, since I am working weekends at Alvin's Donuts and am making $1.25 an hour.

"OK," I say to Doug, who then shakes my hand. We all start to laugh, laughing at our own situation, where everybody wins something, fair and square. It is not until Tuesday of that week that I have some time in the afternoon to go to the bank and get the $800, leaving about $1000 in my account. Not bad for a poor kid from Harwood Heights. Tuesday evening I go over to Doug's house. I go over the car, a 1964 black Beetle with an orange interior, which is spotless as I expected, and turn over the $800. Carol gives me the signed title, and gives me hug. I am very happy to have her car. Over the years Doug has provided many things in my life for which I am very grateful. This experience is yet another example of Doug's caring and concerned nature that has provided me with many good times and memories.

It is now late October. I get home from school in my black Bug and park it in the street, so I do not block my dad in, and enter the house through the front door. My mom is in our living room, working on her school work while she is baking bread. When she bakes bread the whole house has a wonderful aroma. It smells that way this day. Before I leave the living room to go upstairs, and even before I say hello to her, she says in a measured voice, "I have some news for you." I expect that someone in the family has died, or some other family problem. She tells me that Doug and Carol have moved to Burlington, Wisconsin, where Doug will serve on the city police force. I know about Burlington because I was there with my Aunt Myrtle when I stayed with her last summer at Lily Lake, Wisconsin. We went there for supplies and food. I liked the place a lot. I feel somewhat sad, since the last time I saw Doug and Carol was when I bought her black Bug. I am happy for Doug, because I think a policeman is the perfect job for someone like Doug who cares about others, is a good person, and follows the rules. These are the important things that Doug lived by and taught us in our lives when we were together. This night I say a prayer that they will be happy and blessed by God in all the things they do. With all of the things in my life that are fast approaching, I never see or hear from Doug again.

Roy J. Solofra   Douglas S. Lind   Kenneth F. Kline

New Police Officers Anxious To Serve the Community

Force at Full Strength . . . .

Three recent additions to the Burlington Police Department fills the vacancies created late last year by the resignation of three officers. According to Police Chief Walter Gabriel, this brings the force up to full strength once again.

A thumbnail sketch of these new officers follows:

KENNETH KLINE

Kenneth F. Kline, 24, Rt. 1, Burlington, began his duties with the Burlington Police Department on November 1. Kline is single and has been a Burlington-area resident all of his life. A 1961 graduate in the class of 1961, Kline joined the U.S. Air Force, serving four years. Prior to applying for the police department position, Kline worked as a mill man at Lavelle Rubber Manufacturing Co. in Burlington. Asked why he chose law enforcement work, Kline said, "I felt that I would like to be of service to the community."

DOUGLAS LIND

Douglas S. Lind, 23, resides at 313 E. Market Street, Burlington, with his wife, Carol. Lind is originally from the Chicago area and a 1960 graduate of Maine Township High School. Lind, like Kline, is a U.S. Air Force veteran. Following his discharge from the service, he was employed by United Air Lines at O'Hare Field, working in the ramp service department.

RAY SOLOFRA

Ray J. Solofra, 34, lives at 172 N. Kendrick Ave., Burlington, with his wife Joanne and their seven children, a U.S. Marine veteran, Solofra has been employed for the past 5-1/2 years as a driver-salesman for the Pepsi Cola Bottling Company in Kenosha. Prior to this time, he operated a tavern and grocery business in Fell Lake.

All three of the newcomers are very enthusiastic about their new job, and are anxious to provide the best service possible to Burlington.

County Court Is Busy Place

Fined $10 and sentenced to 150 days in the county jail under the Huber law after pleading guilty in the Racine County Court, Burnech 2, to a charge of operating a vehicle after his driver's license had been revoked, was James Marvin Welfoltz, 21, of Racine. Welfoltz was arrested, Nov. 14, by the Burlington Police on E. Jefferson St.

Forfeiting $30 bonds in Branch Two were Michael F. Battista, 44, Lake Geneva, speeding, (40-25) Milwaukee Ave., Jan. 2; Raymond J. Meyers, 31, Rt. 3, (bus 933.9), speeding, (40-35) Main St., Jan. 2; and Victor H. Ruback, 23, Rt. 3, Box 271, illegal mufflers at S. Pine St., Dec. 17; Bonds of $20 were forfeited by David Nickas, 31, Galesburg, Ill., speeding, (40-30) on W. State St.] Jan. 5; George J. Urquhart, 22, Kenosha, speeding, (48-30), Jan. 7; Kenneth G. Komen, 30, Evanston, Ill., speeding, (43-30) on S. Pine St., Jan. 8; Carlyee E. Gandt, 36, Wilmot, speeding, (43-30) on S. Pine St., Jan. 5; David H. Middlebeck, 29, Bristol, speeding (47-30), on S. Main St., Jan. 9; Henry M. Kilinski, 51, Chicago, speeding, (44-35) on W. Chestnut St., Jan. 7; Donald W. Parker, 20, Racine, speeding, (44-30) on N. Chestnut St., Jan. 8; William H. Cury, 46, Darien, speeding, (44-30), S. Pine St., Jan. 10; and Charles W. Roessman, 19, Waterford, stop sign at Kane St. and Jefferson St., Jan. 31.

Fined $35 after pleading guilty to speeding charges were; Alfred D. Drew, 26, 235 Reynolds Ave., (45-30) on S. Pine St., Jan. 10; and Ralph W. Bohensch, 40, 125 Schumann St., (53-35) on Milwaukee Ave., Jan. 3.

After pleading guilty to a charge of failing to stop at a stop sign at S. Pine St. and Jefferson St., Jan. 3, Marvin W. Kradl 42, Waterford, was fined $15; also fined $15 was Wayne E. Zarudnik, 26, New Berlin, an illegal U-turn, at W. Chestnut St., Jan. 21.

Farewell, my good friend and mentor.

CAROL'S NOTE

I am very grateful to John Snell, Sr., for bringing the adolescent and high school years of my late husband Doug Lind to life. John and Doug were boyhood friends, living on the same block in Harwood Heights, Illinois, and John's retelling of adventures with Doug opened a window into a chapter of Doug's life I wouldn't have otherwise known.

Doug's mother, Mary, and my grandmother, Elaine, were friends as girls, and remained close friends throughout their lives. Doug and I seldom saw each other as children, but I have a photograph of him holding my hand in front of his boyhood home when I was about two and he was five. We reconnected during my junior year of high school when he was home on leave from the Air Force for a family funeral. We fell in love and were married two years later, raising four children (Peter, John, Bryan, and Maria) during our 42 years together, until he lost his battle with cancer at the age of 65.

As John remembers his friend Doug on the pages of *Doug Times*, he mentions many traits of Doug's personality he respected and admired that were evident throughout Doug's adult life. He loved and served God, our country, his family, and friends. He was our community's first Officer Friendly, a master craftsman, artist, humanitarian, historian, loving husband, father, and grandfather. We were very blessed to be Doug's family.

Doug Times is a reminder of how one life can touch and impact so many other lives. I have no doubt that when Doug came face to face with his Lord and Savior, Jesus Christ, he heard the words, "Well done, good and faithful servant." [Matthew 25:23]

As you read *Doug Times*, I hope it rekindles fond memories of a good and faithful friend in your own past.

~Carol Lind King

ABOUT THE AUTHOR

JOHN THOMAS SNELL, Sr. was born at Augustana Hospital in Chicago, Illinois on a cold snowy day. He grew up with his mother, father, sister, and Calico the cat in Harwood Heights, just outside Chicago, until he enlisted in the US Army.

Snell graduated from Luther High School North in 1964. He earned a Bachelor of Architecture degree in 1970 from the University of Illinois (Chicago) and a Masters degree in Administrative Science from The Johns Hopkins University in 1983.

Snell served in the army from 1971 to 1974 achieving the rank of Sergeant (Specialist 5). He lived in Louisiana, Missouri, Virginia, and Washington, DC during his years in military service. While in DC, he was a member of the Engineer Strategic Studies Group. After leaving the service with an honorable discharge in 1974 he moved to Columbia, Maryland.

While studying at the University of Illinois, his undergraduate thesis in structural engineering was published jointly with two other colleagues and presented at the Canadian Conference of Applied Mechanics in 1971. Snell went on to become an architect and a professional engineer with active licenses in ten states, and has designed buildings in the USA, Ireland, and Mexico. He has also had several articles on pharmaceutical engineering published in professional journals.

Snell later moved to Connecticut in 1982 and to Florida in 1995. He is currently a practicing architect and professional engineer in Florida. He and his wife Mary live outside of DeFuniak Springs, Florida on lakefront property in an attractive house which he designed. Snell is the proud father of three adult children and grandfather of two sensational grandsons.

Snell is a motorcycle enthusiast and has owned many motorcycles over the years. He rides only Triumps and Yamahas. He is also a model train buff with a fine collection of HO gauge, N gauge, and garden trains.

Snell speaks one language, English, fairly well.

Made in the USA
Lexington, KY
26 November 2019